THE DAY TO DAY GUIDE OF TREKKING EVEREST BASE CAMP

And What Isn't in the Guide Books

Ta Hiron

This guide provides all the information I couldn't find online, collates the information I could, adjusted and added to with information from the trek itself.

My partner Dom and I trekked over weeks in August and September, with a tour group; therefore, there is reference to this particular season and type of experience. I have included what I learnt along the way for other seasons and various ways of getting there.

No matter how you choose to get there or in what season, this guide is the guide I wish I had. I collated so much useful information on the whole experience and in preparation for the trek that I got voted by my tour group as the most organised! Let my hours in planning make your trip, as it did mine, much less stressful and lighter through effective planning, packing and knowledge.

Of course, this is the planning, the items and the approach that worked for me. You may find you want or need different things based on you, your trekking methods and the season you travel in. Of course, each year the trek itself with what is offered, what accommodation there is and each individual guide's knowledge, changes the experience.

Better prep equals less stress and a better experience. Take only what you need, leave at home what you don't so you can spend more time enjoying one of the most amazing hikes this world has to offer.

I am a Life Coach and Nutritionist but this is information on my trek. It is not and does not replace medical advice. You should always seek personal medical advice from your Doctor before taking anything, going on this trek, what medication you should and shouldn't take and in all circumstances.

We made a video of our trip that is on YouTube, the link is HERE, or you can search for the video's title: 'Everest Base Camp August-September 2017 Dom & Ta.'

Table of Contents

CHECKLISTS

To organize beforehand

- Book tour if applicable

- Book flights

- Book transfers if using

- Organise Currency, beforehand if possible

- Passports

- Nepal Visa

- Medications, Vaccinations, First Aid Kit

- Emergency plans/funds

- Insurance – that will evacuate you from the mountain. We used Covermore but always call and check they will helicopter you off if need be

- Consider actives and book accordingly either side of the tour in Kathmandu or the like

- Prepare and research your packing list and put together a 'To Buy' list you can start purchasing from as sales come up

- Bring 2 passport sized photos for your TIMS pass or organise it beforehand.

To Take

Goes with notes in Packing and Set Up to further explaining some of these items/choices

- Worn in hiking boots * See the section about Clothing & Shoes
- Waterproof jacket/raincoat
- Waterproof pants
- Camp shoes/crocs
- 4-5 pairs of socks, aim for 1 new pair every 2-3 days
- Quick-dry T-Shirt
- Hiking lightweight long sleeve shirt
- Hiking Pants/Shorts - zip off pants are best
- Undies x10 – personal preference and you may be able to hand wash or pay to have washed
- 3-4 sports bras
- Evening Pants
- Thermal Shirt
- Thermal Pants - if cooler months
- Down Jacket
- Mid-layer Jumper – can double as evening jumper
- Hat - preferably with neck flaps/legionnaire style
- Neck warmer/Buff
- Gloves & Ski Gloves if in Winter
- Sunglasses (consider second pair if you are prone to losing or breaking)
- Head-torch
- Water purification method: SteriPen/UV light voted best in our group as you get sick of chemical tasting water with others.

- Spare Batteries for any devices such as UV light, torches, etc.

- Nepal Charger and cables for devices

- Solar Charger securable to backpack

- Cheap nail brush to clean shoes after the trek to get back through customs

- Sunscreen minimum of 50 SPF

- Lip Balm with SPF

- Microfibre towel

- Any desired altitude/heart rate/pedometer type device with chargers

- First Aid Kit

- Biodegradable wet wipes, enough for 2-3 per day for your 'shower' and opposite morning/even face wipe

- Toilet Paper x2-3 rolls each

- Tissues

- Bag locks x2 each person

- Hand sanitizer

- Snacks/Chocolate

- Water bottle to fill up and treat water in before topping up your bladder

- Water Bladder

- A day back 30-40L

- Waterproof cover for your day pack

- Camera and/or any video equipment you want to take

- Power Bank for electronic devices - can use the solar charger to replenish

- Sleeping Bag - recommend taking your own

- Sleeping bag liner

- Aqua Water Purification Tablets (back up to UV light)

- Diamox if recommended by Doctor

- Antibiotics - bowel and any other medication recommended by Travel Doctor

- Vitamin C/Berocca

- Electrolytes

- Ural – for Bladder infections and to Bi-carb load, more info later on that

- Gastrostop

- Antiseptic Cream

- Mintec - 100% peppermint tablets that greatly aid everyday stomach upset

- Travelcalm or travel bands for anyone prone to travel sickness, or you can just take dried ginger to eat as well as wear the travel bands

- Cold and Flu tablets – we didn't use but a few on the trek did get sick

- Foot tape – prevention, I didn't use but try it out if you are prone to blisters

- Band-Aids - management

- Panadol, both ibuprofen and paracetamol

- Magnesium Oil and/or Tigerbalm

- Money belt or similar

- Hiking Poles - can easily buy there

- Ear covers - cold winds

- Beanie

- Hair ties

- Hair Brush

- Spare plastic bags - (dirty clothes, shoes, wet clothes, daily rubbish)

- Small foldable bowl for washing face brushing teeth

- Nail file

- Passport

- Visa

- Sweatband if you use these

- Insect repellent for lower areas

- Easy to read books - don't bring anything too heavy on the brain

- Toiletries

- Small mirror

- Ziplock Bags for travelling internationally with 100ml toiletries

- Throat Lozenges

- Gaiters if going in snow season

- Earplugs – for sleeping when noisy

- Eye Mask

- Knee brace/strap/Patella Strap - the small strap that sits just under your kneecap

- Map – buy there if you like to follow along or are not in a tour group

- Travel Guide – if you like to follow along. If not in a tour group this is recommended.

- 5x Envelopes to put tip money in

- Notebook and Pen, if you are a note taker

- Trip Notes from tour or alike if provided.

- String Up clothesline

- After sun lotion

Make a 'To Buy' list of what you don't have as early as you can to start gathering as sales come up.

What we wish we had/had more off

- More savory snacks

- We didn't take a nail brush to clean our shoes and paid more there for one

- Others only took a cap (hat) and looked on very enviously at the legionnaire flaps on our hats after days of max UV 12. People did get their ears burnt and blistered with sunscreen on and reapplied

- Others didn't take cold and flu tablets and got sick

- Others didn't take Vitamin C and had to ask for some of ours

- Others didn't take a solar charger and again commented on ours

- Others didn't have any knee braces and after 2 weeks of up and downhill had sore knees and commented on this as great prevention.

- Many in the group who used chemical water treatments had to buy Tang to help with the chemical taste

- After sun lotion - most got burnt

What we didn't end up using that was suggested

- Waterproof pants, only because it didn't rain enough but this would have been handy if it had

- More than 2 pairs of trekking pants and tops – you really will re-wear

- More than 1 lip balm

- Sarong or Swimmers - the thermal pools noted in the guidebook are not on the EBC trek

- A metal water bottle to put 'free' boiling water in to heat up your sleeping bag. All places charge for even a bottle of boiling water. We had appropriate sleeping bags that didn't need further warming. If needed, the liner adds more warmth and sleeping in your thermals also adds warmth. Most places we stayed at had blankets as well.

- We didn't use our sleeping bag liners as we were plenty warm

- I took a disposable camera as back up I didn't use

- We found the pace of the trip good on our feet and therefore didn't develop any blisters so didn't need prevention tape or band-aids.

- Overshoe rock protectors

- Duct tape/electrical tape for any repairs

- Salt for leeches - we didn't see any but on other treks in lower areas of the region we heard there were many

- Books that were too in-depth were too much with all that was going on. We didn't read any books we brought except the light easy to read ones.

- Toys/Gifts - our guide discouraged giving gifts to children. I ended up leaving a little gift in each Tea House I stayed as a thank you instead.

- Gators/Quagmires - we didn't walk in any snow on our trip

- Sheewee - seriously I just squatted the few times this was needed. After all, if you use it, you have to clean it!

- Alarm - I bought a small battery-operated alarm clock but our guides woke us when needed, or we used our phone.

- Tea bags - I read you could bring your own and ask for hot water to make it cheaper. It hardly saves at all, and most of their tea is made with real, fresh ingredients.

- Cards - there are games in some tea houses, but we didn't feel up to games but many did

- Map - we rarely referred to it with our tour leaders

- Travel Guide

- Probiotics

- Water filter - we didn't take it and didn't miss it. Sometimes there are particles in the water you get at tea houses you could filter out. Might depend on where you get your water. We were told to always ask in the tea house for it from the kitchen, not to fill it out of basin taps.

I purchased the Lonely Plant's book Trekking in the Nepal Himalaya. As I was with a tour group, I didn't find this book essential. I read it more beforehand to get a sense of the trip but not much on the trip as I was there enjoying it with my guides telling me what I needed to know. If you are not with a tour group I would highly recommend purchasing this for the trip, or if you want in-depth information before you go on the landscape, route and country. The book allows for planning various routes and gives tips on side hikes.

THE TREK - DAY BY DAY

We made a video of our trip, the link is HERE, or you can search for the video's title: 'Everest Base Camp August- September 2017 Dom & Ta.'

Photos of the journey are on my facebook album found HERE.

Getting to Nepal - Day 0

Our trekking tour was from 26 August to 9 September. We left Australia on the 24th August, arriving into Kathmandu on the 25th via Bangkok.

We arrived at midday on the 25th August in Kathmandu, the day before our tour started. We hadn't been able to source Nepali Rupee (NPR) before the trip, with it not offered at the usual exchange places. I know it is often better rates to exchange money in the place of origin; however, I don't like the risk of exchanging all my money with the possibility of a scam.

In the Kathmandu airport, I noted locals were lining up at a freight exchange for cash and decided with it in the airport and used by locals it had a good chance of being legitimate and a decent rate. We exchanged our combined $1,300 AUD for NPR. At first, we got wads of 1000 NPR notes. I explained we needed smaller notes, as I had read these may be hard to exchange in the mountains. The attendant grumbled, but I explained I was going to the mountains and he gave me wads of 500 NPR, and these were wads!

Get 500 NPR Notes if you can but many on the tour easily exchanged 1000 NPR notes at the tea houses, it is the smaller trek side vendors who would need smaller notes.

We had booked transfers from the airport to the hotel. We tipped our driver 500 NPR. While not in today's exchange rates our guide told us to think of 500 NPR like $5 USD, as the locals did.

Back at the guest house in the safety of our room, we assessed the wads of cash. I had read that, like all cultures, clean notes are preferred with old, dirty, ripped notes often being offensive if offered. However, we didn't have a choice; we got the notes we got.

We spent a good hour carefully prying out big stables from the notes and decided to sort the notes into a range of dirty to clean. We planned to try to use the dirtiest first as if these were refused we had more to draw on rather than if it was our last note and it was refused. We only had one instance after a meal out in Kathmandu where we handed over some very dirty ripped notes I felt terrible about, that he looked at for a few moments but accepted.

The restaurant we went to was on street away from Kathmandu Guest House (KGH). It was up some stairs, called the Himalayan Cafe & Restaurant. It was a good meal. I recommend it if you can find it.

Day 1 - Kathmandu

We met our Intrepid tour group at 2 pm at the KGH. We were briefed by our leader and provided duffel bags. The duffel bags can be filled to no more than 10kg. These are what our porters carry for us on the trek to each new night's accommodation. In addition to this, we have our day pack which for the flight from Kathmandu to Lukla can weigh no more than 5kg, a total weight of 15kg. As water is heavy were advised to leave our bottles and water bladders empty, we could fill these in Lukla. It was advised to pack our batteries into our check-in duffel bags as well as our trekking poles.

With a free afternoon in Kathmandu we planned to walk to the Monkey Temple after Durbar Square, but the square was further away than expected and we ran out of time. I would suggest paying and getting a guide and/or taxi.

When you go out, have your buff with you. It is dusty, and you won't fare well breathing a lot of that dust and air pollution which is why you may need the lozenges.

Day 2 - Kathmandu to Phakding

We had a 6.30 am flight out of Lukla which had us arise for collection at 5 am from the hotel.

Bags are weighed at the airport. You will need to pay for extra weight if it is allowed. The duffle bags are checked in, and our daypack is carry-on. It is cheap to pay for extra but not always allowed.

We had some water before we left Kathmandu and enjoyed breakfast on arrival in Lukla at the cost of 650 NPR for a meal and drink.

Lukla is 2,840m, and the flight was 45 mins in a small plane. Take earplugs and enjoy the scenic views.

In Lukla, we met our porters, all local boys from the area. We learnt that they come in as porters and can move up to assistant Guides and Leader Guides as their English improves and they gain trekking knowledge and confidence. Each porter in Nepal can carry up to 70kg. We even saw some Nepali on the trek carrying over 100kg - too much. Intrepid only allows each porter to carry 2 duffel bags, at a maximum combined weight of 20kg. Another reason to ensure you don't overpack your duffel.

The boys tie two duffel bags tightly together with rope and then with a thicker band, place this over their forehead to carry the bags before shooting off to the night's accommodation. This packing tightly with ropes means anything that can get squished will and does. Take any liquids with you in your day back to prevent them being squeezed out or at least put any products in a zip-lock bag in case it does get squished. They are fast and strong, either up in the morning and gone before you, as soon as the bags are ready, or, if they leave after you, they zoom past you on the trail as you are left panting on struggling with your 5kg day pack.

For our arrival into Lukla, the weather was warm and muggy. We wore T-Shirts in the 2,000-3,500 meter range. You warm up quickly hiking up a hill.

The toilets along the trekking paths were long drops often consisting of a tin shed with a wooden floor that had a hole cut out and some leaves in a bin on the side to place on top for composting. You need your own toilet paper everywhere. I didn't see any track side toilets near Base Camp but only had to find a rock to hide behind once. Often there enough villages you pass through to find a toilet where you stop for tea.

Our first night's accommodation was at the Mountain Resort Teahouse. It was plush we learnt, with our own shower (cold water only) and a toilet per room. A western flushing toilet too!

Along the way we were able to have our water bottles topped up for free at Tea Houses we stopped at for Morning Tea breaks. We would always sterilize our water.

Snacks were easily purchased in Kathmandu, Lukla, and Teahouses along the way. Prices increased a little as you went higher. The main options were Pringles and chocolate in either Snickers, Mars or Bounty. We were glad we brought our own snacks to have more variety and healthier options.

Most of the trekkers in the group who are on Diamox have commented on experiencing on-off tingling of the hands and feet as we do, sometimes even our face.

As we travelled off the back of monsoon season that tracks weren't very dusty. We had occasional on and off light rain showers throughout the day.

We are taking a Berocca and electrolytes daily. I am also taking Ural to aid the lactic acid burn which isn't much anyway with the increased blood flow that comes with altitude. What we didn't anticipate was the need for a small bottle to mix these with water in each day. We kept a water bottle we were given earlier by our transfer to use.

I wore a Fitbit which had a daily calories goal of 2,260 which I would only reach on very long walks back home. On this trip, it went off daily and earlier and earlier in the day as we got higher and higher. Today I hit the calorie goal at 4.30pm.

We didn't feel hungry at dinner, a symptom of altitude. We forced it down and luckily didn't experience this again until above 5,000m.

Lunch today cost me 550 NPR.

This was approx. a 3-hour hiking day.

For our Acute Mountain Sickness (AMS) symptoms today Dom gave his a 3 out of 10 (10 being the most severe) due to a loss of appetite at dinner. I rated a 5 with a headache and loss of appetite.

Day 3 - Phakding 2,610m to Namche Bazaar 3,440m

Yesterday and today we easily drank our 4Ltrs of water with the hiking and hot weather. I found it easy to drink my first litre before I was out of the room in the morning. A bit of this was used for my electrolyte, Berocca and bi-carb (Ural) mix.

When we arrived at our accommodation each evening, we would change out of our wet sweaty hiking clothes and have a 'wet-wipe shower' where we clean ourselves with cleansing wet-wipes before changing into our comfy, dry camp clothes.

In these lower areas, there have been only mosquitoes at sunrise and sunset.

So far, we haven't seen a lot of the mountain tops due to low cloud. The mornings are our chance to see the mountains then the cloud comes in over the day, often with a little shower around 2pm.

A few got sun-burnt today despite full cloud cover and wearing sunscreen. Our lightweight trekking shirts with full-length sleeves have been a good option with the hot sun and sweating.

We crossed 2 suspension bridges today, one being the highest we cross in the trip. We hear in peak season you can wait in line up to 30 minutes to get across.

For lunch, I had Veg-Fried Potatoes 450 NPR, with a Masala Tea 100 NPR.

Gifts for local children have been discouraged by the tour leader.

Today was a 7-hour hike day. After breakfast, we set off and reached Namche Bazaar, 3,400m, at 3 pm. Goal calories were reached by 2.30pm.

We are being trekked at quite a slow pace as this helps our bodies acclimatize. We have rest breaks after most steep sections at which the group is encouraged to drink water.

Most tea houses sell snacks and toilet paper but Namche Bazaar is the last place to buy a range of things you may need.

Our accommodation offers a warm shower here for 400 NPR. We treat ourselves and have a warm shower. I also do a quick hand wash of some clothes just as I spot a no hand washing sign! It wasn't the best move as with the rainy weather our clothes took 3 days to dry. I had to pack them up wet and rehang at the next place even with the tip of wringing them out, then laying each garment flat on our microfiber towel, rolling it up and wringing it out again.

The lodges all have rooms with 2 single beds. Only 1 along the whole trek had a room with a double bed. The single beds are plain with a mat/carpet on them. Some have a bit of a mattress. They all have pillows and blankets. We opted to lay in our sleeping bags on top in case of bed bugs or the like, though others have slept in the bed with no problems.

Most tea houses have shared toilet, shower and basin facilitates.

We had our first Nak cheese pizza here. Yak is the male and the female who makes the milk is a Nak. It was delicious and highly recommended with the lodges making even the dough from scratch. It has an aged cheddar taste. The pizza was 550 NPR which we shared with some Onion Rings for 400 NPR. They had a deep-fried mars bar on the menu here for 330 NPR which we shared for dessert. I highly recommend. I also had some Ginger, Lemon and Honey Tea for 180 NPR - this is delicious and made with freshly sliced ginger, honey and lemon juice. It is settling for the stomach on the trip and ordered by most of the group often.

We have had a few power outs in the tea houses and are in the habit of putting our head torch around our neck as we get into the lodges each day.

We are advised not to fill our water bottles in the room (on the rare occasion you get your own basin) or from hallway taps. Ask for it from the kitchen.

I had read in my research before the trip you can get free hot water each night to either put in your water bottles or to have brought your own tea bags to save money on tea, but this hasn't been the case. This Teahouse, for example, has 1L of hot water at 200 NPR.

AMS symptoms today we rated ourselves at a 1 each.

Day 4 - Namche Bazaar

We spend another night in Namche Bazaar for an acclimatization day. We hike 9.7 km on our acclimatization hike. There are no rest days. We always have an acclimatization hike if we are stay more than one night.

For breakfast, I enjoyed porridge with honey that tastes like toffee, 400 PR. It was one of the best breakfasts over the trip that many often ordered with it being filling, simple and tasty. Some places serve it with honey so check before adding as it may have sunk to the bottom.

Our acclimatization hike today took 4 hours. It was a sunny day that was very hot. We hiked up to a place called Syangboche which had a tea house at the top. We were advised of a very high UV exposure of 12 today. Most got burnt, even getting blisters on their ears. Through the clouds, we got our first view of Everest today which was spectacular.

Following the end of monsoon, the ground is green with many wildflowers.

We had no rain today.

I hit my calorie target at 4.50pm.

Our guide advised us today that the Tea Houses don't often get much money for our accommodation as it comes with the expectation we are buying meals there. Therefore, it is helpful and appropriate to buy meals at the Teahouses we are staying at. Part of the reason I prefer tours is they take you to places they know are preparing their food correctly. I was happy to buy there for ease and getting a stomach bug on a trekking trip when you are out hiking all day if something I was keen to avoid.

There is no killing allowed on the mountain. So, from Lukla and beyond there is no fresh meat. We are advised to eat vegetarian at all teahouses after Kathmandu, even those close to Lukla. Chunks of meat are carried in on foot for as many days as it takes to reach their destination. Often locals pass us on the trail with these chunks of meat filling their basket with only a plastic cement type bag as a cover.

We are advised the milk used in our Masala Tea was most often fresh cow or powdered milk down low but could be Nak milk up higher. I tried some Nak milk Masala. It was tasty without much difference in flavour.

Most snacks people are eating are chocolate bars for energy and having soft drinks at the tea houses. I am enjoying my muesli bars and taking energy from ginger and honey tea, keeping a chocolate bar for only every few days.

You can haggle a little in Namchee, if you buy a few things, but of course these aren't wealthy people, please pay a fair price.

Bringing Tiger Balm and Magnesium oil have been worthwhile. A few in the group have come and sought our Tiger Balm for twinges in muscles. We have been putting one or the other on of an evening.

In the lower areas, the 'yaks' are a crossbred hybrid of a cow and a yak, with the pure Yaks only found in the higher altitudes. You see their noticeable difference as you ascend with the yaks having a larger form and much more shaggy coats.

Not all in the group are on Diamox yet. When someone says they aren't sleeping well, they are often the ones not on Diamox. Over the trip 2 of the boys stayed off it and fared well, one of which had been at altitude before. We wanted to give ourselves the best chance of success in reaching Base Camp so took it as the Doctor advised, from Kathmandu onwards rather than try to hold off.

You can get your clothes laundered here for a few hundred NPR as one girl did, returned warmly from the dryer in a few hours. Make sure if you do this it can be put in a dryer. Other places I noted had clothes on the line, and it just kept raining on them.

Dinner tonight was Vegetable Spring Rolls for 500 NPR. These are 1-2 large spring rolls that fill the plate with a side of potato chips.

I have noted those that have ordered toast with jam, that it doesn't come out with butter. If you want butter, you have to ask for it.

Our sleeping bags are rated to minus 10 degrees and have been more than enough in these end-of-summer months, no liner or thermals needed.

AMS symptoms today Dom rated a 5. I rated a 6 with our acclimatization hike leaving us breathless. Dom also had another headache. I could hear Dom breathing much heavier than usual in his sleep.

Day 5 - Namche Bazaar to Phortse 3,810m

Breakfast today was 2 scrambled eggs, 400 NPR and a ginger tea, 100 NPR.

Lunch was Dhal Soup, 350 NPR, with ginger tea, 110 NPR, at Mongla, 3,973m. It was an 11 km hike to get to lunch over 4 hours. I enjoyed another ginger tea to help settle the stomach.

With the uphill, I have made a point of taking full, deep breaths to ensure I get reasonable amounts of oxygen and exhale completely.

On the incline, Dom had a thumping AMS headache today which he took some ibuprofen for and was fine after.

We hiked a total of 17kms today, from 8am to 5 pm with plenty of breaks.

For dinner, I ordered a Dhal Bat, 500 NPR, with a Ginger, Lemon & Honey Tea, 110 NPR. The Dhal Bat is a bottomless meal that will be topped up as much as you can eat in any place you order it.

There are no western toilets at our accommodation tonight, we have the full experience. After our first night with the plush flushing western toilet, the rest have been manual flush western toilets. There is a large barrel of water is beside the toilet which you are to take a scoop from with a jug that sits in the top, to pour the water into the toilet yourself to flush. Always take your toilet paper and hand sanitizer with you.

We are laughing amongst the group at managing to squat tonight with our sore hiking legs. I didn't think of it until after but taking in a hiking pole to shorten and hold onto would help if your legs were really unsteady.

Today we rated our AMS symptoms as a 4 each with on and off headaches.

Day 6 - Phortse to Periche

Dom had a persistent headache last night and took aspirin to help. I had an upset stomach after dinner and had to take a ginger and a peppermint tablet before bed. It felt like a normal tummy upset but over the trip I realized the Dhal Bhat was just too much for my stomach.

We left by 8 am today. Once you get into the accommodation of an evening, there isn't much to do between arrival, dinner and bed. With our bodies going through so much, we are finding our minds don't really want to concentrate on much. Most nights we don't even feel like reading the books we brought. We are often asleep early and appreciate feeling fresh the next day.

We hiked today from 8am-4.30pm. It was a hard hiking day. We hiked 3-hours until morning tea, followed by 1-hour until lunch, then 2-hours until reaching the tea house at 4,200m.

The tree line ends at about 4,000m. The lack of trees contributes to the lower amounts of oxygen in the air.

I have a sore throat today, and Dom has had a bit of an upset stomach. We have both had headaches which are mostly there as soon as we hike up an incline. A headache mostly fades at rest.

I have easily drunk 5L of water today with the big walk. Those not reaching their quota are mostly those without a hydration bladder in the backpack. The bladder makes it much easier to drink while you walk and keep little bits of water coming in regularly rather than big gulps just when we stop.

One guy in the group who is struggling ended up developing a bad throat/lung infection. Towards the end of the day, the guide was carrying his back as he slowly walked along. Such an effort in his condition to power on. We had two doctors in the group who looked after him and had him inhale over steaming water a liquid tiger balm for a few evenings. The liquid tiger balm is local and is passed around a bit with people putting it on for headaches and sore muscles.

While we don't have much of the lactic acid burn, we do have fatigue in our muscles with the multi-day hiking. But it is all manageable and we don't feel any of it is out of our physical ability. The whole groups is soldering on well.

It was quite cold after lunch today and at rest.

Out of 10, Dom gave today's difficulty a 6.5 and I gave it a 7.

We are finding we are getting ravenous throughout the day, starving by morning tea with everyone tucking into their chocolate bars to see them through to lunch.

For breakfast today, I had a vegetable omelet at 450 NPR, with Ginger Tea for 100 NPR.

Lunch was Vegetable Fried Rice, 500 NPR with a hot Tang, 100 NPR.

Dinner was Potato and Cheese Mo Mos (Dumplings), 450 NPR and Lemon Honey Tea, 150 NPR.

AMS symptoms today we rated ourselves at a 3 each due to breathlessness on the hike.

Day 7 - Second night in Periche

Another hot day of t-shirts and shorts but with lots of sunscreen on every speck of exposed skin. It was a bit cooler yesterday at rest, but today in full sun it is hot making the incline a bit more of a challenge.

I have switched to leggings now. The last few days I have worn my short sleeve shirt and yesterday with it being a bit cooler, I wore my lightweight long sleeve shirt.

The hike was up to 4,576m today. We hiked 7.5kms over 3.5 hours. Our shortest hiking day of the trip.

For lunch today, I have a hash brown with cheese and egg 650 NPR, and a Masala Tea 150 NPR.

We have heard that another Intrepid hiking group leaving the day before yesterday couldn't fly into Lukla due to weather. This will shorten the time they have to hike when they get here, and therefore they may not reach Base Camp.

The difficulty of today was rated by Dom at 3 and me at a 4, due to the breathlessness I get at this altitude while hiking. I am even breathless if I do a bit of talking as I did in my video here you will see if you watch the YouTube video.

Each evening our tour leader briefs us after dinner on the next day's hike as to getting up times, travel distances, what to take in our day packs, as in if we expect rain, how many of liters of water to leave with etc.

We are advised tonight that tomorrow we cross a glacier where the steel bridge got swept away in this summer's monsoon. Another temporary one has been made, and the guides will be on hand to help us cross. We are reminded to take it all slow with our hiking by the saying 'slowly gets the money'.

It has been a great group dynamic, and all are supporting each other. If anyone mentions anything they are feeling off with most others are pulling out this remedy or that to aid them.

I had Sherpa stew for dinner tonight for 550 NPR. It was delish and very hearty. We also ordered Veggie Mo Mos not realising the stew would be so hearty as we didn't really need the Mo Mos.

AMS symptoms today we rated ourselves at a 3 each due to breathlessness on the hike.

Day 8 - Periche to Lobuche 4,920m

The masala tea, like a less spicy chai, is a drink I am ordering often. Only 1-2 places had a very bland version of it. Sherpa stews are different at each tea house but always hearty full of rice and/or pasta and vegetables. With Mo Mos you get 12, which a plate of makes for a smaller meal or a well-shared entree on a day you are starving. Another hearty meal is fired potato, you can get it with vegetables or cheese, or both. Some Tea Houses have also got pasta dishes with a tomato sauce or vegetables. Pizza is always good, and for breakfast the potato hash with an egg or cheese has been a good choice if you like a big hearty meal to start the day. I have stuck to a lighter vegetable omelet or porridge for something easier on the stomach of a morning. If you have a sweet tooth and like bread, try the Tibetan bread. It is akin to a doughnut which you have with jam.

Today's walk was up a valley crossing over a mountain and up another valley to Lobuche. My calorie goal went off at 2.30pm showing the extra work our body is doing at these higher altitudes on even the slower paced walks.

Dom and I are feeling good with the altitude at present with walks on the flat an easy stroll, but extra effort required on the incline has me puffing and needing regular gulps of water.

Obviously, if someone is naturally a faster walker comes up behind you, you move aside and let them pass on the trek. We have come across a few people that don't make way. It isn't a race. We all have naturally different walking paces, and we like to walk at our own pace, so please move aside if someone comes up behind you on the trek.

Our guides remind us of the importance of this track etiquette especially when a local is carrying up one of their heavier loads. When you are coming towards each other on the track, the rule is to make way for the heavier load. Also, make way for the Yak and stay mountainside.

As I was very hungry, lunch today was veggie fried potato with cheese, 680 NPR and a masala tea 120 NPR. I note the Sherpa stew here is 450 NPR and porridge is 400 NPR with an extra 50 NPR for honey on it.

After we reached our destination today, we were given the option of an hour hike to see a glacier and reach 5,000m for acclimatization. Despite arriving in full cloud cover again, 3 of us did the extra walk. Not many take up these additional hikes now. It really depends on how you are feeling with fatigue and altitude. We have been fortunate to be faring very well, so I am giving myself the little push to make the most of being here.

In the group a flu is going around as well as a few stomach upsets and headaches with the acclimatization.

It was cool today. I hiked in my quick-dry hiking pants, a wool long-sleeve base layer with my lightweight, quick dry long sleeve and a rain jacket. Also, a fleece headband/ear cover and a buff on our neck. Many wear the buff on the neck up the back of the head and over the chin. People have done this for warmth in the cold and for sun protection on the hot days if they only brought a cap for a hat.

We have been fortunate to have blankets available at every tea house. Most are pretty well stocked up on them, but I imagine in the high season they all get handed out. We hear in peak season there aren't enough rooms and some tourists end up having to sleep on the floor or benches in the dining areas. This tour guarantees us a room.

We have our food orders for dinner taken when we arrive and are told the time of dinner will be ready. The Intrepid tour group has made so much convenient and easy like this. All the guides and assistant guides wait on us. Whatever we want, they take our order and usually deliver the food from the kitchen for us. This helps the tea houses too. They take breakfast orders the night before and as soon as we appear in the dining area in the morning, even if it is before breakfast time they bring us our ordered drink while we wait for breakfast. They tally up our orders at each teahouse during our 1-2 night stay, and we settle the bill just before we leave.

It is all cash in the mountains. Have all your money with you, wear it on you at all times. This isn't such a concern in the low season where it is often just our tour group in the tea house, but I imagine in high season there are people everywhere. Best to lock your rooms each time you leave and even then, keep your cash on you.

We have seen many stray dogs from down low to up high. Often one will follow the group for a few days. A few in our group fed it. Our tour leader said the issue with feeding these dogs is they will stay with the group as they trek up high and end up in the national park where they pose a threat to the wildlife. We explain this to those that fed the dog who understand now and stop. We had another dog higher up follow us for a few days with no encouragement.

We are having to get up most nights to go to the toilet with all the water we are drinking. It isn't avoidable and better than risking worse symptoms of AMS from not having enough water.

The tea house we are in tonight, very excitingly, has not only western toilets, but, drum roll… a flushing one!!! Very plush! We hear in the depths of winter pipes can freeze and so can the toilets. I am not sure how that is all managed in peak season. Winter here means clear views, so the frozen pipes and crowds is the price you pay. We have been happy to settle on less clear views of the mountains, that we often get up early for to have tea houses all to ourselves and no lines, no waiting.

We reach EBC tomorrow and have to cross a glacier to get there. Today's hike was quite mild despite altitude slowing us down. We rated it a 4 out of 10 each. My calorie goal still went off at 2.30pm.

We have an early start tomorrow, no doubt to get the views before cloud cover comes in. Breaky is at 5.30am, and we leave at

6am. Getting up for early mornings has been easy, as we are in bed early weary from the walk and with not much else to do. We hike up to Gorak Shep in 3-hours, have lunch then hike up to Base Camp and back to Gorak for the night at 5,140m, being our first and only night staying above 5,000m.

AMS symptoms today we again rated ourselves at a 3 each due to breathlessness on the hike.

Day 9 - Lobuche 4,900m to EBC 5,364m to Gorak Shep 5,140m

A very overcast start to today but it cleared up for amazing views at Base Camp. We walked 20 km today, hitting my calorie goal by 2 pm and in total burning 3,213 calories for the day. We started at 6 am and got to our evening accommodation at 5 pm.

Base Camp is just an area of rock. I had heard it is just a pile of rock amongst the rock or an area of rock and it really is. Nothing special that gives it away apart from the flags and the handmade sign.

Crossing the glacier was more like crossing a big rock quarry or rocky canyon bottom. There were sections you could see the ice underneath and being we were there in the warmer months we could hear it cracking and dripping. Part of the group got separated as a rock slide occurred when we walked across. The leaders have all this prepared for, they are split up amongst the smaller groups we have split into and regroup us throughout the day.

Thanks to our leader's advice and guidance our entire group made it to EBC which we hear is the case about 50% of the time. We ran into groups ascending as we descended who were eating meat and one guy boasted how he didn't need to sterilise the water.

If anyone needs to turn around due to illness, a leader has to go with them leaving fewer leaders for the larger group. Of course, illness and AMS can be out of your control and I care deeply about getting someone back to safety in these circumstances but increasing the risk of your health for some macho reason isn't a game to play in these parts. This is a place to follow guidance every step of the way from eating and drinking as guided, through to our pace and routine in preparing our bodies at every step. And despite illness, flu and fatigue in our group, as all followed the guidance of our wise leader we all made it.

Our time at the EBC site was fantastic. There were only 2 other smaller groups, so we spent a good hour taking all the photos we wanted, enjoying the moment over a snack break there and curiously checking out what was left of the ice blue glacier to the side what sat on top of the rock half melted.

The group was quite fatigued having had the big moment come and go. We are finding that while we experience much less of the lactic acid burn in the muscles than when not at altitude, some are feeling it now on a good incline.

Lunch today was a vegetable soup, 400 NPR which at this lodge, unfortunately, didn't have chunks of vegetables in it which I was hoping for. This is the difference I learn between a soup and a stew.

Sherpa stew was my dinner tonight at 650 NPR. Dom is having a tomato and cheese pizza which our guide tells us is all made fresh, including the pizza base, on the premises as well as the mo mo pastry.

AMS symptoms today Dom rated at a 6 due to a headache. I rated this day a 5.

Day 10 - Gorak Shep 5,140 to Kala Patar 5,400 to Orsho 4,040m

Today is our biggest day of the whole trip for those that take the before breakfast hike to Kala Patar. Only four of us in the group got up for this at 4 am. It is noted as the best view of Everest in Nepal.

We headed off in the pitch black with our head torches. We crossed a small flat area then hiked straight up. At every 15-20 steps straight up at this altitude, I was gasping loudly for air. I would stop catch my breath and continue. I was the slowest in the group of 4. My guide was excellent, telling me we were doing well, it wasn't a rush and to just keep taking it slow. I was glad to have an external voice of reason that was monitoring me to save me relying on my own inexperienced judgement in this situation.

Dom and I went up halfway to 5,400m as I was struggling. Dom could have made it, but when our guide said the view from where we were was as good as it was up the top I decided that I was happy to wait here for the others to return. Dom was happy to stay with me.

I really struggled following a night where I barely slept for 3 hours. Sleeping above 5,000m didn't allow for a comfortable night's rest on top of the fatigue of the journey.

At these altitudes, there is only 50% oxygen in the air, and our body are down to 80% of their usual holding of oxygen, so we are gasping for air more to make up our shortcomings but only getting half of what we normally do with each breath.

After the early morning hike to Kala Patar, we joined the rest of the group for breakfast back the tea house who were eager to hear about the experience. We then set off to Orsho descending over 1,000m. As a result of the descent, today was the last day I took Diamox. Dom kept it up a bit longer to ward off symptoms. The whole group noted in the evening, after having dropped so much altitude, how much easier it was to breathe and how much better we were feeling. We arrived into Orsho at 5 pm, making it for the four early morning Kala Patar hikers a 13-hour hiking day.

We seen many Yaks today which we often have to pass through the heard of. The guide advised they can charge so keep moving and don't get too close.

The smell of burning Yak dung at the tea houses is pungent and burns your eyes if the smoke gets near them. They load up the central heating fire burners with the manure of an evening which is welcome for the heat, not for the smell.

So far about 1/3 of the tea houses we have stayed at have squats, most being above 4,000m. Other western toilets mostly require the manual flush which is interesting to learn the right pouring technique to have a number two move through and not just bob around in the water - the trick is to pour the water directly only it quickly.

There are often no sinks or a couple that had no running water for hands, so lots of sanitizer and wet wipes are needed.

The group concurs that no one slept well above 5,000m with lots of broken sleep and many midnight toilet breaks required. Those willing to laugh at the whole experience have all noted how gassy the food has made us - all that dhal! We laugh that often what is perceived as a number two is just gas. The altitudes slows your body processes down and this, in turn, ferments the food creating more gas. A suggestion would be to keep the bread and pasta type carbs to a minimum if you experience this and stick with the stews, omelets and alike. We are taking a peppermint tablet that consists of pure peppermint oil, daily to just help with our stomach to be as preventative. I have also taken charcoal tablets to help with the gas, and we have taken between us 3 Gastro Stop tablets over the trip. I took one after just a slightly loose movement to prevent anything further from developing on that day's hike.

The daily hikes have been well paced with tea houses and outhouses at regular enough intervals up until 4,000m, but there are enough rocks to find shelter often as I did once. Still better than having a raging headache from not drinking enough water so don't drink less to avoid this.

Dinner tonight was fried rice, 450 NPR with ginger, lemon and honey tea, 180 NPR.

We rated the difficulty today, the biggest day of the trek as a 7 from Dom and a 9 from me.

AMS symptoms today Dom rated a 5 due to Nausea and breathlessness, and I rated a 6 feeling dizzy, fatigues, and severely breathless on the Kala Patar hike.

Day 11 - Orsho 4,040m to Tengboche 3,840

A three-hour trek today which was down into a valley and up the other side with a very unwelcome incline. We are back under the tree line.

We stay at a monastery tonight which we are going to watch their ceremony at 4 pm. This is a Tashi Delek Lodge and Restaurant. It is the most expensive on the trip. But this price brings very welcome stable electricity and an extensive menu. They have a sign up saying oxygen services are available.

For lunch, there is a veggie burger on the menu. A burger - get out of town! The veggie burger is 700 NPR, and a masala tea is 200 NPR. The burger was something that would be regarded as quite plain back home but to get a burger here was heaven.

We have commented thus far in that we have been happy with our clothing choices. Dom notes he would have only bought 1 pair of zip-off pants and just worn them more often, but we are pleased with our numbers of socks and undies that allow us a fresh pair every other day. If anything, Dom would have also bought 1 extra quick-dry, lightweight long sleeve top in place of s t-shirt as this can be worn any day and offers sun protection for his arms. Also, we would have bought wool base layers which are supposed to smell less, but none of these have been missed.

I haven't used my beanie as I use the buff as a headband or my fleece ear cover which is sufficient with the hood of my jacket. We still haven't used our sleeping bag liners due to enough warmth, but this would have possibly been a good idea to keep the sleeping bags cleaner, not that they got dirty but no doubt you sweat in them over the course of a night.

The days are warm again now that we are under 4,000m. In the season we are here we only wore our puffer jackets above 4,500m.

We are told in the Himalayas women are not to wear shorts above the knee and neither male nor female are to wear singlets. Leggings/tights are ok.

A tip is to make sure you wet-wipe between your toes and all your feet with them in shoes all day, this helps prevent blisters.

We are told the entire walk to base camp is 118 km round trip, excluding side hikes, so you end up doing probably 150-160 km we estimate, with our acclimatization hikes.

Dinner today was a pizza, 900 NPR, and a hot chocolate, 300 NPR. Today I hit my calorie goal at 7 pm.

AMS symptoms today we rated at a 2 each due to headaches on the hike up.

Today's difficulty was rated as a 3 from Dom and a 4 from me due to the last hill to get to Tengboche.

Day 12 - Tengboche 3,840m to Monjo 2,800m

Prices I have noted on the trip are

- 400-600 NPR for a shower, mostly cold

- 200-400 NPR for a full charge of your phone

- Wifi 250MB for 400-600 NPR - which is often a sim card type thing and not always available but much more than I expected it to be.

You are asked not to wash clothes by hand in the sinks. Some places offer a bucket of water for washing for 50-200 NPR.

We are now very sick of chocolates for snacks and want something savory so bought some Pringles which are in most shops for 400-600 NPR.

Some are showering now we are back in Namche Bazaar with the warm shower, but we have figured why bother with no clean clothes and still more hiking! We have found it much easier to be un-showered on the hike than expected. There was no noticeable difference on the track the next day between those that had showered and those that hadn't.

We crossed 3 suspension bridges today and walked back through the pine forest.

AMS symptoms today Dom rated a 1, I rated a 2 based on breathlessness.

The difficult of today was a 6 for Dom and I with quite a bit of uphill.

Dinner was Veggie Spring Rolls, 450 NPR and a hot choc, 120 NPR.

The veggie spring roll hasn't always come with chips but mostly. We had lunch at Namche Bazaar today. I got prawn crackers 400 NPR, Veggie Mo Mos, 500 NPR and a Masala 120 NPR.

I have selected an apple pie for breakfast tomorrow at 450 NPR. This is a rare treat to be found.

Day 13 - Monjo 2,800m to Lukla 2,830m

Today, the last hiking day on our trip is both down and up over 5 hours.

The difficulty of today we both rated at a 5 with it being a hot sunny day that included inclines after many days of trekking.

It is our last planned night here, and we have a big group dinner that includes all guides and our 7 porters. We all chip in to shout them dinner and a drink. They are teenagers and in their early twenties. They are very shy. We are told as it is isn't usual for them to get to talk to the tourists. We are told many tour companies don't let them interact and they struggle to go against these first lessons despite having been invited to join us.

AMS symptoms today we rated back down to a 1 each with slight headaches and a little breathlessness.

Day 14 - Lukla

Our flight out of Lukla is delayed. We had a 6am flight out and now at 8 am we all sit waiting. Both Kathmandu and Lukla airports are closed due to weather but could open later today. Since our arising at 6am the clouds have grown thicker. There is still hope the fog could lift and we watch commenting on seeing it getting clearer one moment to getting thicker the next.

Some in the group are getting very agitated, and we are reminded of a flight in May this year that flew in these conditions, a cargo plane that crashed at the end of the runway killing the 2 pilots and stewardess.

Our connecting flight tomorrow, out of Kathmandu into Bangkok feels like we booked it too soon now.

The second night in this accommodation takes away the joys of the hot shower.

As the cloud continued to close in there is a discussion on the possibility of the airport opening for tomorrow, but it doesn't look promising and we discuss getting helicopters in to get us out. There is the possibility of the airport opening in which case if we have booked the helicopters we have to go still and pay the $300 USD to take the choppers.

The helicopter's price is $500 USD, but we would get money back from our Lukla flight that was cancelled, and the tour company is willing to chip in a little too which is fantastic. This brings it down to $300 USD each. This is still an off-peak price. We hear it can get up to $1,800 USD in peak season with the competition of people trying to get out. That is if it doesn't go higher in the bidding war.

We decide to book the helicopters, the whole group. They will come in to get us regardless of if the airport opens or not long as good enough weather permits.

Day 15 - Kathmandu

We are waiting this morning, a quick breakfast had, and all are packed up awaiting the signal to head to the helicopter pads.

As I write this, I get the call it is time to go. Dom, I and 4 others are on the first helicopter out determined by who had the soonest departing international flight out of Kathmandu. We head off with our bags, carrying our duffel which is ours now the porters have been relieved. The extra time we have stayed on our Leader and assistant guides have stayed to continue to serve us with meals etc. This I believe was above and beyond what is required of them, not paid. We are more than happy to manage our own duffel now.

The tour company has organised a transfer from the airport taking us directly to the hotel. Our guide has notified them of our international flight time, and they are doing what they can to get us there on time.

We get back to the hotel and get the suitcase we left behind. We ask for a meeting room or the like to do transfer our clothes out of the duffel into our suitcase, but hotel is not so accommodating, we have to do our clothing shuffle in the hotel lobby. We don't have time to feel embarrassed by this and make the shuffle just in time for our transfer to the airport. All transfers were organised in conjunction with Intrepid. The absolute beauty in this is that they were fully aware of our situation and had been arranged to arrive in line with our current situation. I didn't have to make any calls about this. We make the transfer and get to the airport with an hour to spare!

We make our resort check in and have the best shower and dinner and an uninterrupted 14 hours of sleep, waking up to an all-inclusive breakfasts buffet we enjoyed three courses of!

Additional Hike Notes

This trek reminded me we can do so much more than we think we are capable of. This trek sure had some hard moments, but over-all, it could be accomplished by many ages and fitness levels. If you want to see it and can walk you can probably do the trek with the right guidance.

When I returned, so many fit and able people just said they could never do what I did. I couldn't imagine the obstacle they had put up in their head, but I reminded them they could, it was really just one foot in front of the other. But I guess what is more important than the physical is the mental decision to do this. However, don't risk any AMS type symptoms, seek advice early.

Overall the trek was easier than I had anticipated but the morning trek up to Kala Patar is the hardest physical thing I have now done.

Please don't accept plastic bags when purchasing, carry or use your own as rubbish is a significant problem the country struggles to handle.

We found it hard to take it all as you are so focused on the day-to-day organising of your water, your AMS symptoms, food, toilet stops, upset stomachs, weather, etc.

Remember:

'Stay mountainside, and give way to the Yak'

Keep the prayer flags to your right.

Walk clockwise around the many painted rocks. Spin the prayer wheels clockwise.

Check with your hotel, but it is common to leave your larger suitcase at your hotel in Kathmandu. As we were on tour we were provide our duffel bags at the hotel to place what we needed for the trek into and leave the rest there.

Clothing & Shoes

A lot is personal preference, for example, I wore a Speedcross 3 Salomon Trail Runner as I know I prefer a low-cut shoe and feel restrictive in boots. However, Dom is the opposite and wore Zamberland hiking boots with ankle support. I got away with the trail runner due to the summer months, I don't know you could do this in winter as they wouldn't be as good in the snow. But for me, a wet foot for a day or two was better than blisters every day.

I ended up bringing:

- 6x undies

- 6x socks

- 4 sports bras

- 2 quick dry t-shirts

- 1 lightweight merino long sleeve

- 1 long thermal sleeve

- 1 thermal short sleeve - didn't need this

- Shorts to wear over my leggings but I didn't wear these. I thought this would be more appropriate, but many just wore leggings.

- 1 compression leggings which could have just been normal leggings

- 1 quick dry pair of pants

- 1 mid layer jumper

- 1 rain jacket and rain pants

- Evening socks and track pants

- 1 vest

- 1 puffer/down jacket

Each day you need only what you need for on the trek each day if you are using a porter.

I took in my day pack:

- 2 litres of water - topped up at tea houses along the way

- Camera and any electronic devices I needed for the day

- Solar charger if I needed to charge for the day with Power bank to top up

- Snacks

- Cash

- First aid kit and medicine

- Raincoat, warmer layer or puffer when higher

- Hat

- Sunscreen

- Sanitizer

- Toilet paper

- Notebook to make notes at lunch

We prepared before we left to have only a day pack knowing most of our gear would go in our duffel bags the sherpas would carry. We still needed a decent sized day bag to fit in our rain gear, coats, snacks, up to 4ltrs therefore 4 kg of water etc.

There is a 15kg maximum per person on the Kathmandu to Lukla flight for your duffel and daypack. You will pay extra for more weight which isn't an enormous cost but isn't always an option.

Don't leave your shoes outside your room or tent at night, they can go missing.

In setting up your day pack, have a tighter waist strap that sits the majority of the weight on your hips, not your shoulders which will lead to headaches and an upper back ache. Have your top chest strap done up just enough to stop the bag swaying side to side. Be conscious when you put your bag on where the weight is, shoulders or waist and adjust accordingly.

Notes on some of the gear

- Hiking boots & Clothes * See section Clothing & Shoes

- Headtorch - brought a smaller one and wished I had more light when I did the Kala Patar hike.

- Water purification method: SteriPen/UV light voted best in our group as you get sick of chemical tasting water with others.

- Any desired altitude/heart rate/pedometer type device with chargers - I used a Charge2 Fitbit, and it worked a treat. It was interesting to see my heart rate change and how much sooner in the day I hit calorie targets as we got to higher altitudes. However, it didn't really add any extra value to the trip, and I feel I could have easily gone without as well.

- Toilet Paper x2-3 rolls each – you could easily buy there and along the way but I wouldn't count on it in high season. I took it as I didn't want to spend my time shopping for these things if I didn't have to, to spend more time enjoying where I was.

- Bag locks x2 each - I left a lock on my suitcase in Kathmandu and also put a lock on my duffel bag. We used number lock ones, so we didn't have to worry about losing the key. We probably didn't need to lock our duffel bags since we had so much of the spaces to ourselves, but I still would and definitely in peak as the porters take your bag and just leave it in a common area of the tea house until you arrive so people have access to it. Dom had a lock break, and we were glad we had a spare.

- Snacks/Chocolate - take a good mix of sweet and savoury.

- Sleeping Bag - recommend bringing your own. One guy in the group hired one and found it quite damp, he had it out by the heater trying to dry out. Not ideal in the cold and yuck!

- Antibiotics - bowel and any other medication from Doctor - we specifically took bowel antibiotics as well as general. There aren't medical services on the mountain, you have to be prepared to be self-sufficient and consider what is likely. We are glad we didn't need it but if we did this would have been the difference between possibly soldiering on or heading home early.

- Vitamin C/Berocca, Electrolytes - we took these daily and felt they helped us.

- Foot tape - prevention - we didn't need it and didn't get any blisters but should we have felt the rub I would have been glad to have it.

I made sure I could easily access my camera which was my iPhone while on the trek. I did this by purchasing a new case that had a belt clip attachment that I clipped onto the waist clip of my trekking bag. This way I was quickly able to get a quick photo without holding up the group.

We also took a solar charger which we could clip onto our day packs.

TRAINING, TREKKING & RECOVERY

Upon commencing this trek Dom and I were regular all-day hikers. We hadn't done multi-day hikes, but we had done regular 5-8 hour hikes, up to 8-10 hours in our peak. Dom regularly rides/mountain bikes as well.

In the 3 months prior we walked at least once per fortnight 3 months out, increasing to once per week 2 months out and also did a couple back to back day hikes in the month prior.

We rested for 1.5 weeks before the trip to allow full recovery for a fresh start.

In saying all that, some people hadn't trained at all in our group, no doubt they had a harder time, but they still made it. Don't be discouraged, you can do this.

If you can muster up the energy do some stretches when you get into camp each day to help your muscles. Hold the stretch for 30 seconds. We would lie on the bed and do leg stretches most days.

Your body as a 30-45-minute window after exercise that if you eat within it, it will maximise reabsorption of energy into your muscles. Have a protein/carb snack as soon as you are at your evening place of rest for better energy the next day. We often ate jerky or nut bars.

Soon as you get into camp also try to drink the remainder of water quota for the day to get it through your system well before bedtime. You will still need water during the night so have it nearby. Be prepared to get up during the night.

Bicarb loading - for lactic burn reduction. This can cause a gastric upset so practice at home first and look up more information if you are interested in consultation with your doctor. Bicarb before exercise can neutralise your body's production of lactic acid, in turn, reducing the lactic burn. I tried taking a sachet of Ural for an easily dissolvable form in the mornings before the hike.

Carb Loading - You can bulk up your body's stores of carbohydrates to draw from in the days before the trip. This is easiest done in the 1-3 days before you start trekking by enjoying high carbohydrate meals.

During your trek keep your protein up - think jerky and nuts. Jerky isn't something I would advertise having there with their sacred view of cows, but I kept some packed away for a snack at the end of a days trek that I wish I had bought more of.

INSURANCE AND FLIGHT INFORMATION

Register your trip and all trips with SmartTraveller or alike in your country

We used Cover More for insurance. The critical thing to check as I did via a phone call was if they would rescue me from the Everest Mountain in the areas/altitudes, if I broke a leg or got sick. They said they would, but this could have changed, always do your own research at the time of travel.

We didn't end up getting out of Lukla as per the schedule. The initial day intrepid had booked the Lukla to Kathmandu, the Lukla airport was closed due to heavy cloud. This continued through to the next morning, and the whole tour group opted to get helicopters out, so international flights were not missed. We managed to get the cost of the helicopter back on our insurance as the flight was cancelled out of Lukla. We had to get a letter from Intrepid confirming that flight was cancelled. I was glad to have gone through a travel agent that made contact with her representative in Intrepid for this letter. It took some time and a few chasing emails with the insurers, but we got out money back.

If you are taking your own trekking poles, as we did, either have them in your check-in luggage or if you are taking them on as hand luggage you need to have the metal ends covered with the plastic stopper. I got a run around by security and almost lost mine due to not having my stoppers on, on a different trip.

We took and it was agreed amongst the group as the best option for water purification a Steripen with lithium batteries (which lasted the whole trip) and as a backup should we have any problems we had Aquatabs.

It is discouraged to consume alcohol or caffeine at altitude. Alcohol and altitude don't mix. Additionally, it further dehydrates you which is what can bring on AMS.

Caffeine isn't recommended mainly due to dehydration. However, one guy on our trip enjoyed a black coffee each morning with no problems. He had altitude experience before and knew his limits.

They carry up all the meat. Nothing can be killed in the mountains, it is killed elsewhere and walked up in a sack for as long as it takes to reach their destination which could be over a week away. We could smell this as it passed, it was quite pungent and not meat I would eat unless I wanted to test out my bowel antibiotics. Our guide recommended we don't eat the meat on the trek, and the whole crew happily ate vegetarian, and all made it to Base Camp.

We had to drink 4-5L of water per day which wasn't a struggle until the last few days coming back down. This amount of water reduces the likelihood of AMS, and it also gets more oxygen into the body.

Tips to drink 4-5L of Water per day

- Drink 1L on rising - this enables you to use the accommodation facilities after breakfast
- Drink 3L on the trail

- Drink 1L in the evening, best done soon as your accommodation is in sight or on arrival to get as much through your body system before bed.

MONEY AND SPENDING

In August 2017 the exchange rate was AUS $1 = 75 NPR.

We took our spending money and an emergency $500 USD which we used $300 to get out.

There are plenty of banks in Kathmandu you can get your money exchanged at. I was quite nervous with this, while advised that as long as it is a bank, not just any old shop when you are there, you see that it is hard to distinguish a reputable bank from a dodgy shop. You could ask your tour guide or hotel where is the best place to go. We got our money exchanged at the airport. I did this as I noted many locals were lining up at an exchange if the locals use it, it is a good sign, be in food, money, etc. We took our AUD and had it exchanged.

Ensure you advise your bank of your travel plans in case you use your credit or debit cards abroad.

In AUD our costs for the whole tour and travel, each were:

- Flights return $1,218

- Our flights could have been cheaper, but we opted for flights going through Bangkok which we stopped at for a resort recovery on the way home - I highly recommend.

- Intrepid Tour $1,572

- We managed to get the normally priced $1,895 tour on one of the Intrepid Specials - and for those that got the discount for being a member of Kathmandu shop in Australia, that unfortunately no longer is available.

- Insurance $204

- Visas (Nepal) $110

- Transfers $51

- Accommodation $76 Kathmandu for an extra night before the tour for a room (not each)

- Vaccinations $500 I specifically went to a Travel Doctor and wasn't disappointed just quite a bit poorer.

- Spending $650 This included meals, purchases, tipping and for the extra day in Kathmandu - You could spend less or more depending on you. The tour group recommended $450 USD for meals which would have been enough, but you would have needed an extra $100-150 USD or more for tipping depending on you and if you are tipping just a porter or like us a tour leader, assistant guides, porters and any transfers/taxis taken.

- Emergency $500USD - In case of emergency we were asking to have hidden $500 USD, and we did use it. This allowed us to get helicoptered out to make our international flight.

Tipping

It was recommended to give no less than a 50 NPR note where possible to prevent insults. This isn't always possible, and you have to give what you have which I deemed better than nothing, I always tip as I can, but sometimes you get a lift before you have your foreign money or as we seen in our group circumstances that had us stay longer than expected in Lukla ate into others tipping fund.

It was recommended on this trip in 2017 that appropriate tipping was:

$3-5 USD per day for a group leader

$2 USD per day for a guide or assistant guide

50-100 NPR per day for porters

Our guide recommended we take 40,000 NPR for the whole trek for meals at about 30,000 NPR per day plus tipping. I thought this was a little light on in my experience, but it really depends on your spending as I guess this would cover meals, but not if you got extra snacks, toilet paper, etc. You can see some of my meal orders in day by day listing to help you work this out.

We ended up giving in tips all we had left but would have like to have given more, but our extra night ate into these funds which are a consideration, that you could be stuck over there and need to allow more meal money if so.

Helicopter - We paid $300 USD for our helicopter as this was subsidised by our tour company and reduced by the pre-purchased flight from Lukla back to Kathmandu which we got $130 USD back on. However, this is a low season price. Expect to pay, as noted by in the Lonely Planet up to $1,800 USD if you want a helicopter flight out in the high season, if you manage to get one as those willing to pay more will be the ones who get the flights first.

WHY A TOUR GROUP

Why Intrepid - so many examples have been given throughout this book. They go above and beyond and sort out with local knowledge all that is needed to make it the best stay possible. I don't want the stress of getting lost so remotely in a foreign place so for me a real holiday isn't worrying about this. I love Intrepid tours as I get plenty of downtime, local intel and guided from a-z without worry and told how to prepare.

If you do a tour check out their trip notes and read them in detail. We were surprised how many in our tour group had not read the provided trip notes and therefore were unaware of some necessary information.

SEASON & TEMPERATURES

Out timing had us do the trek just before peak season as August is still monsoon and September is when the trekking high-season takes off - we commenced 25 Aug and finished 9 Sept. This made for hot days, but we got cold higher up.

Our Seasonal temperatures given were 6-16 degrees in August to 5-19 degrees in September.

In August from Australia, the time difference to Kathmandu is 4 hours behind. Google your country 'time difference Nepal to xx'.

TOILETS

There were adequate stops planned at tea houses etc. for breaks and toilet breaks. Finding a rock to hide behind only happened once and wasn't a big deal at all. There were mostly western toilets at our tea houses however they required manual flushing with a bucket of water. Squats higher up which with more fatigued legs made for quite the challenge. Toilets along the trail were very basic long drops but all in all better than expected. I wouldn't like to experience the 1-2 toilets in a full tea house in peak season sharing with a few hundred people. We got used to having tea houses to just our group! So if going to peak be prepared to line up or get up and go early.

Always have your toilet paper and hand sanitise on you. There isn't always running water for your hands.

Take enough toilet paper to see you through should you get the runs!

ALTITUDE, AMS & OXYGEN

A headache, nausea and fatigue are common symptoms of Acute Mountain Sickness (AMS). It these symptoms persist descend to lower altitudes, consult a leader or guide.

AMS can affect people above 2,000m. Our guide told the story of one person as soon as they touched down in Lukla experienced symptoms that had to send her home.

Ensure you tell whomever you are with about any pre-existing medical conditions. This is not a place for trying to tough it out. Knowledge of such conditions enables better success in helping you reach the top safely. Additionally, it can affect the safety of your team if guides are required to take those down due to AMS or other conditions they are not effectively talking through with to the guides. The tourists that die are often those that try to keep up with a group and don't voice their conditions.

At our maximum height of 5400m, there was only 50% oxygen in the air, and our body's capacity was down to 80% oxygen. Resting heart rates were often around 100 beats per min, maybe a bit less while sleeping.

We fared pretty well with AMS aided by taking Diamox an altitude medication. We had good advice to start the Diamox in Kathmandu, initially to allow the diuretic phase to pass (lasts a couple days) and then to also have it in the system. Those in the group that got AMS the worst were not on Diamox and their symptoms reduced once they took it. Only 2 did the full trek without it and fared ok. AMS symptoms are a pounding headache, nausea, dizzy, breathlessness. I got a headache day 2 or 3 in, quite early but not as bad after that. Dom got a headache much higher, and it came and went over a few days. Mostly it would kick in when you were hiking up but subsided when at rest. We both had one night where we weren't nauseous but didn't want to eat and had to force down dinner. But above 5000 you are a bit off in general. I was very breathless on any incline after about 30 steps, while for Dom was quite nauseous.

The day after base camp where we had slept at 5200m, there was the option to get up at 4 am to hike up to 5400m to watch the sunrise behind Everest. Only 4 in the group did it. With the high altitude, I managed only a few hours sleep. The hike started in the dark and went straight up a mountain. I was gasping heavily every few steps, felt dizzy and really struggled. It was the most challenging thing I have done, and I must admit I was a little scared at the full experience of it. It was worth it but such a challenge physically and mentally. I kept on under the guidance of the tour leader who had my safety under close watch. That was our biggest day as we hiked until 5 pm making it for the 4 early risers a 13-hour day. It was our turnaround day so apart from the morning was all downhill.

Diamox - This is a medication and is to be prescribed by your Doctor. It is noted as a diuretic, my Doctor advised this is only for the first few days, commonly thought by trekkers to be the case while on the medication for the duration. However, this is more likely the 4-5 L of water you need to drink per day at altitude to help prevent AMS. Due to this, I started my medication a few days earlier in Kathmandu to allow the diuretic effect to pass while I was near facilities. I didn't feel the effects of it to be much of a bother. My Doctor advised, but please check with yours, that I was able to cease it as soon as I was feeling well on the descent. I had read otherwise that I had to get back to the altitude I commenced taking it before I could stop.

The benefits of the medication I felt are that it helps you breathe, those not on it sometimes reporting to awake during the night gasping for air.

At the end of the tour we felt we fared well, Dom even raced one of the guys in the group on the last section back through the first gate at Lukla, however, the following few nights at our resort in Bangkok we step 13-14 hour nights for a few nights. I would recommend keeping this mind for your own recovery, that you can have a few lazy days with long nights of sleep.

NEPALI WORDS

This wording was provided by our Nepali Guide

Hello: Namaste

Thank You: Dhanyabhad

Welcome: Swagatam

Please: Kripaya

Very Good: Dharai Ramro

Beautiful: Sandar/Sundari

How are you: Tapain lai cast chaa?

I am fine: Malai Chanchai Chha

Yes: Ho/Hunchha

No: Hoina/Hudaina

It's: Chha

Not: Chhina

My Name is … and I am your Leader: Mero naan…Ho Ra Ma taipan ko leader hu

See you later: Pachhi Vetaula

ELECTRONICS

Store electronics in your sleeping bag at night to prevent large battery losses in the cold.

I used my iPhone 7 plus for all photos and video. I only needed a battery top up once over the two weeks as I put by phone in 'low power mode' in the battery settings and on 'Airplane mode'. I also turned off 'background apple refresh' in the Settings-General. I now do this for any multi-day adventures and use approx. 10-15% of battery per day with taking photo and video.

For the latest tips or for those relevant to your device simply Google 'improving device 'X' battery life' or 'cut back on 'X' device battery use' or similar.

Nepal power sockets take the 2 round peg plug 230V/50Hz or the three-round peg 230V/50Hz. This is only available when there has been enough daylight on the trail for the tea house's solar to charge and have spare. Don't expect it always to be available and where available expect to pay around $5 USD per phone charge.

We took solar chargers.

Internet

$5USD for a small amount of data in most places, again in low season this was readily available, high season this might sell out quick so ask soon as you get in if you need it.

REGISTRATION & CERTIFICATES

Our group organised our Trekkers' Information Management System (TIMS).

You will get either a blue or green one. Blue for Group Trekkers 'trekker/s using local facilities/expertise such as Trekking Guide/Support Staff and all the pre-booked facilities' and green for Free Individual Trekkers 'trekker carrying own luggage and bearing all the liabilities and responsibilities individually.'

At one of the main entry points into the National Park, there is a sign on the office where you can get your certificate. This is the only place I saw this available, therefore if you would like a certificate of completion for your trek, pick this up at the first place you see it when you exit via a checkpoint of the National Park.

USEFUL FURTHER INFO

We made a video of our trip, the link is HERE, or you can search for the video's title: 'Everest Base Camp August- September 2017 Dom & Ta.'

Nepal Tourism Board (NTB)

www.welcomenepal.com

When in Nepal:

Nepal Emergency: +977 980 112 3617

Intrepid Kathmandu Local Office: +977 980 112 3617

Photos

Highest Swinging bridge in background

Namchee Bazaar Menu

Hiking along the side of the mountains

Rooms with the two single beds

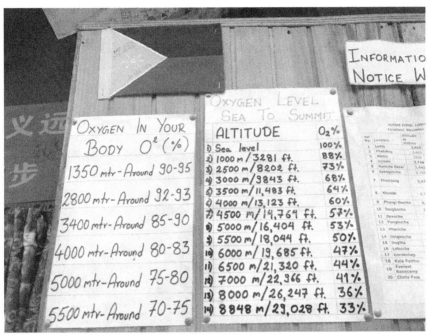

Oxygen signs

The early morning views we would get up for

Inside one of the tea houses living areas

Trekking along the glacier river

Base Camp!

Trekking back down after Tengboche, the cloud coming in.

CONTACT

Website: TaHiron.com – for books, coaching and courses. *Because going out into the world if often about the journey within.*

Facebook: Ta Lisa Hiron

Instagram: talisa83

I am able, at the time of this going to print, to run a coaching session if you want to talk through any of this in preparation or for other trips/travel/life adventures and in general. Email me at talisa83@hotmail.com.

I am a trained Life Coach and University studied Nutritionist. The information contained in this book is not to replace medical advice. You should always seek medical advice from your Doctor.

I hope this guide is useful and you get a few tips. Apologies if I have recounted anything incorrectly. I have done my best putting it all together and hope it paves the way for an amazing trip for you.

I would sincerely appreciate a rating and/or comment for this book on Amazon or Goodreads to help others find the book so they too can access the content for their trek. Would you have a minute you can do that now?

Thank you and safe travels dear friend.

Made in the USA
Las Vegas, NV
07 May 2024

89646011R00049